# Travelling in Time:

*How to Secure Your Future*

# Travelling in Time:

*How to Secure Your Future*

**E.C. NAKELI**

King's Word Publishing

© 2015 by E.C. Nakeli

Published by King's Word Publication

For your questions and publishing needs, write to:

    E.C. Nakeli
    40 S Church st
    Westminster, MD 21157
    E-mail: *ecnakeli@yahoo.com*

Printed in the United States of America

All rights reserved. No part of this publication may be reproduced, stored in a retrieval systems, or transmitted in ay form or by any means— for example, electronic, photocopy, recording—without the prior written permission of the publisher. The only exception is brief quotations in printed reviews.

E.C. Nakeli

To contact the author, write to:

    E.C. Nakeli
    40 S Church st
    Westminster, MD 21157
    E-mail: *ecnakeli@yahoo.com*

Travelling in Time: How to Secure your Future / E.C. Nakeli

ISBN: 978-0-9850668-6-4

    Unless otherwise indicated, Scriptures references are from
    THE HOLY BIBLE, NEW INTERNATIONAL VERSION®, NIV®
    Copyright © 1973, 1978, 1984, 2011 by Biblica, Inc™
    Used by permission. All rights reserved worlwide.


Cover Design: Zach Essama -graphicspartner@gmail.com

Interior Design: Zach Essama -graphicspartner@gmail.com

# Table of Contents

Dedication .................................................................... ix

Foreword ..................................................................... xi

Introduction ................................................................ xv
God's Promise to You ................................................ xvi

## Chapter 1: Seeing the Invisible ............................... 1
The Role of the Holy Spirit ........................................... 2
The Invitation .............................................................. 4

## Chapter 2: Seeing the Invisible One ........................ 7
It Makes the Difference ................................................ 8
He made it easier for us ............................................... 9
David Understood It! .................................................. 10

## Chapter 3: The Power of Your Vision ..................... 15
God's way of empowering .......................................... 16
A driving force ........................................................... 19
For the Joy set before Him ......................................... 20

## Chapter 4: Building Your Future – The Power of Prayer ...... 23
Leave Nothing Unprayed for ...................................... 25
How to pray ............................................................... 26

## Chapter 5: Building Your Future – The Power of Declarations ................................. 29
Watch Your Words ..................................................... 30
Declare the Future ..................................................... 31
In accordance with His plans ..................................... 32
God works in accordance with His plans ................... 33

God is committed to His plans .................................................. 34

**Chapter 6: Building Your Future - Declaring God's Word** .... 37

**Chapter 7: Building Your Future –
The Power of the Right Plans** .................................................. 43
The Power of Planning ............................................................... 44
Our Supreme Example ............................................................... 44
The Power of plans ..................................................................... 45

**Chapter 8: Sow into Your Future** ........................................... 49
The Power of Your Seed ............................................................. 50
The Power of Investment ........................................................... 51
Develop Your Talents .................................................................. 51
Invest in Books ............................................................................ 52
Train Yourself .............................................................................. 54
The Power of Generosity ........................................................... 54
The Power of Sacrifice ............................................................... 55

**Chapter 9: Call Forth the Future** ........................................... 59
Activating Your Future ............................................................... 60

**Chapter 10: Celebrate Your Future** ...................................... 63
How to Celebrate Your Future .................................................. 64
Delight in Your Future ................................................................ 66

**Chapter 11: Surrender Your Future** ...................................... 69
Maintain the Desires .................................................................. 70
Wait for the Lord ........................................................................ 71
Be Flexible ................................................................................... 73
Make Use of Your Opportunities .............................................. 75

**Chapter 12: Step unto the Future** ......................................... 75
A Practical Example ................................................................... 77

**Chapter 13: Avoid Dwelling in Kadesh** ................................. 79
1. The place of doubt and disbelief ......................................... 80
2. The place of delay .................................................................. 81
3. The place of defeat ................................................................ 81

*Table of Content*

| | |
|---|---|
| 4. The place of death and decay | 82 |
| 5. The place of despair | 83 |
| 6. The place of deprivation | 83 |
| 7. The place of disobedience | 84 |
| 8. The place of disqualification | 85 |
| 9. The place of disfavor | 86 |

**Conclusion** ............................................................................. **89**

# Dedication

*I dedicate this book to every visionary, every dreamer, every planner, and all those who see beyond the now into the distant future God has ordained for them. To all those who want to become visionaries, this book is also dedicated to help you take your place among the highflyers of our time.*

# Foreword

I have known E. C. Nakeli for a long time and have always found his books very challenging and inspirational. It was a thoughtful reflective moment when E. C. came to my office to ask if I could be his mentor. My affirmation, after several days, to his questions was based on his humility and readiness to learn. Being a man who likes diligence and truthfulness, I saw that he possessed these qualities.

*"Travelling in Time: How to Secure your Future"* is a book not only for the young in the Lord but for all. Some who started well and made light of their future security ended up in misery. This book gives the necessary steps to follow and end in praise rather than shame! Mental assent has suffocated the

dreams of many Christians and made them blind to the invisible. E. C. says, *"When you cannot see beyond the now, there is great danger that you will compromise the future. The future can only be secured as you see it, plan for it, and pray it through."* If one cannot see the invisible nor see the invisible One God, then his/her future will bring fear. This book brings God on the scene as the only One who holds the future and the One to whom we should be loyal.

In the book you will also find such themes as the power of vision, declarations, prayer, the word of God, right plans, and the dangers of Kadesh-Barnea. It is interesting to see how he captures Kadesh-Barnea as a place of delay, standstill, disbelief, defeat, death, decay, and despair. He strongly suggests, *"In case you find yourself at Kadesh, get up and get out of there before death and decay take over your destiny."* This book leads us to see the future in a different way; many see the future through the eyes of gloom and doom, but this book points to a bright future. We need not fear the future because the Lord has given us adequate understanding of how to reach a successful end. Just follow what is in the book. It has been made simple to read through. I appreciate the power of simplicity, heart-to-heart explanations, and the insight of the subject that God has given His servant.

I feel it is time for the children of God to do and say what the Word of God says so as to guard against the rainy day. What you know today will help you tomorrow. The world is going from bad to worse, arm yourself with the Word. Remember, what you eat now will sustain you in the next hour. Days of difficulties are ahead, tougher times are coming; only those who have travelled in time and secured their future will prevail. You cannot absorb the truth in this book and fail. Thank you E. C. Nakeli for this book.

*Rev. Dr. Pius Forlu*
*River of Life Center,*
*Lanham, Maryland*
*U.S.A.*

# Introduction

Man has always yearned to know what the future holds. Yet it seems God has placed the future beyond the reach of the present. Men travel over land and sea for consultation with powers that be in order to discover what their future holds. Increasingly fortune telling and other satanic practices that claim to foretell the future are drawing the hearts of men and women who want to control the apparently uncontrollable – their future. In the Christian circle today, because the Bible clearly teaches against any form of fortune telling, people are seeking biblical means to know what the future holds by flocking to prophets the Lord has raised in His church.

The questions I seek to address in this book are: Is it possible to travel into your future? Are there Bible revealed ways by which you can get into your future? How can you secure your future before you ever face it?

Mankind's problem has often been the fact that the future has taken him unawares almost every time. From one generation to another men have failed to speak into the future and have it bring to them God's purposes for their lives. Any situation that comes when you are not prepared to face it may possibly not affect you. Those who have learned the secret of getting into the future have learned to take advantage and maximize the opportunities and endless possibilities that come with it.

**God's Promise to You**

The Lord spoke to the children of Israel and said, *"For I know the plans I have for you," declares the Lord, 'plans to prosper you and not to harm you, plans to give you hope and a future.'"* (Jeremiah 29:11)

God says He has a future full of hope and expectations and free from harm in store for you. The writer of proverbs echoes that by saying *"The path of the righteous is like the morning sun, shining ever brighter till the full light of day."* (Proverbs 4;18) In other words the path God has ordained for you is designed

*Introduction*

to get brighter, better and more glorious with each passing day. Your days should be increasingly full of delightful surprises when you learn to get into your future and call forth the things God has in store for you. If you learn to be on the offensive with regards to facing the future, then you will be the victor God wants you to be.

Your background does not matter, it is not very important. What is more important is the fact that you are prepared to face the future and dictate in accordance with God's plan what it brings to you. Do not make the mistake of allowing the future to come to you, take the responsibility to move into the future and influence it with the power of the Holy Spirit and the written promises of God. God's bright future is not for those who meet it passively, but for those who actively, consciously, and determinedly face it before it meets them. In fact you should never allow the future to meet you. Rather get into it and plan it with God before it meets you on this other side of eternity. Join me as we see how you can get into your future, plan it with God, and secure it before it meets you. One thing is sure; you are on a collision course with your future. If you encounter it unprepared, you will be the loser; if you secure it before it comes to you, you are bound to celebrate and jubilate in it gloriously.

# Chapter

# 1

## Seeing the Invisible

In order for you to travel to, and influence your future with God, you have to see the invisible. The future can only be secured when you see it, plan and pray for it. Your future is nothing but the unseen aspect of time. It is that portion of your life that does not exist yet on this side of eternity, but soon will. As we said in the introduction, God has planned a gloriously bright future for you, written in His scroll in heaven, which He uses as the blueprint for your life. However there are forces in the invisible realm that seek to divert it and leave you with something miserable or at least far from what the good God planned for you. If you do not see the future through God's eyes there is no way you can know if what comes to you is in accord with His original plan for you. There are forces in the spirit realm whose only task is to divert and destroy God-ordained destinies. And this can only be done by negatively influencing the unsecured future.

The apostle Paul wrote: *"So we fix our eyes not on what is seen, but on what is unseen, since what is seen is temporary, but what is unseen is eternal"* (2 Corinthians 4:18). Many people's eyes are fixed on what is seen, that is the present. When you cannot see beyond the now, there is great danger that you will compromise the future. Nothing blinds you to your future like when your focus is only on the present.

How can the Spirit of God, through Paul call you to fix your eyes on that which is unseen? Is it possible to see the unseen? Yes, if you look through the eyes of God. For to God everything is in plain sight. Nothing is ever concealed to Him. He created time and separated it from eternity. The future is that part of eternity which is closest to, and will soon become time. This is where the Lord wants you to fix your eyes. You cannot secure what has not been seen.

**The Role of the Holy Spirit**

However, as it is written:
> *"What no eye has seen, what no ear has heard, and what no human mind has conceived"* — the things God has

> *prepared for those who love him—these are the things God has revealed to us by his Spirit.*
>
> *The Spirit searches all things, even the deep things of God. For who knows a person's thoughts except their own spirit within them? In the same way no one knows the thoughts of God except the Spirit of God. What we have received is not the spirit of the world, but the Spirit who is from God, so that we may understand what God has freely given us."*

(1Corinthians 2:9-12)

God wants to show us the good and bright future He has in store for us, that is why He has given us His Holy Spirit. The Holy Spirit did not only come to keep us company and make us feel joyful and peaceful. He also came to reveal to us the invisible, inaudible, and inconceivable things God has prepared for us. This refers to His plans for our future. That is the way we can see the unseen. The Holy Spirit came to give us understanding of what has been freely given us, that is, our bright future in God.

The Lord Jesus Christ said,

> *"But when he, the Spirit of truth, comes, he will guide you into all the truth. He will not speak on his own; he will speak only what he hears, and he will tell you what is yet to come. He will glorify me because it is from me that he will receive what he will make known to you. All that*

> *belongs to the Father is mine. That is why I said the Spirit will receive from me what he will make known to you."*

(John 16;13-15)

The Holy Spirit came to make known to us what is of the Father and His Son, and what is yet to come. These are not just things of eternity but things of the future that affect us as individuals. So to see that future, we must build a relationship with the Holy Spirit who is capable of letting us behold things through the eyes of God. When you are able to see things God's way you become confident and unperturbed in the face of uncertainty and chaos, because you already know the outcome as revealed to you by the Revealer of God's mysteries.

Friend, you can secure your future by getting into it with the Holy Spirit through your declarations and prayers in the power of the Holy Spirit. It's time you desperately ask the Holy Spirit to open your eyes to behold what the Father in His infinite love ordained for you before the foundations of the world.

## The Invitation

The Bible says, *"... Therefore, no one can discover anything about their future."* (Ecclesiastes 7:14) and *"Since no one knows the future, who can tell someone else what is to come?"* (Ecclesiastes 8:7). It is impossible for you to know the future on your own. And it is sin for you to know it through any other means but by the Spirit of God. Throughout the Bible, the Father has continually revealed the future to man because it is His will for man to know what his future holds. He has often given people a glimpse of what the future holds. He did it to Abraham when He told him his descendants will be slaves in Egypt and that they will be as numerous as the stars. He did it to Pharaoh, Joseph, Isaiah, Ezekiel, Daniel, Nebuchadnezzar, Paul, John, and many others through dreams and visions.

That is why because God does not want you to remain ignorant of the future or have it diverted or exchanged by the evil one, He has given you His Holy Spirit and has invited you to Himself to come seek the future. He says, *"Call to me and I will answer you and tell you great and unsearchable things you do not know."* (Jeremiah 33:3). This invitation is for all who are called by His Name. He wants to speak and reveal to you the unsearchable and unknowable future.

The King James Version states: *"Call unto me, and I will answer thee, and show thee great and mighty things, which thou knowest not."* (Jeremiah 33:3). God wants to tell you the inaudible, show you the invisible and give you knowledge of the unknowable. He wants to show you because He knows that seeing is vital for securing the good and bright future He ordained for you. The issue is that many of us have failed woefully to respond to this invitation. For the most part we have ignored it, and therefore the future has taken us unawares and unprepared. The Father, by the Spirit wants to show you great things. He wants to show you mighty things, and He wants to tell you unsearchable things.

Let us pray:

> *"Father, I thank you for the future you ordained for me. I know it is a bright, good, and glorious future. Thank You for the Holy Spirit You have sent to reveal to me the future. Lord, I respond to Your invitation to call on You and now ask that You will, in the name of Jesus:*
>
> *1. Open my eyes to behold the future You have for me*
> *2. Tear every veil that shrouds my view of the invisible*
> *3. Help me behold my future through the eyes of Your Spirit*
> *4. Help me fix my eyes on the unseen*
>
> *Amen.*

# Chapter

# 2

## Seeing the Invisible One

We just talked about seeing the invisible, now I want us to talk about seeing the invisible One. It is not enough to just see the invisible if we fail to see the One who is invisible. The future cannot be secured by just seeing invisible things without seeing the One who holds the invisible together. In the Bible, those who succeeded to secure their future saw both the things and the One who is invisible. Why is it necessary to see the invisible One? Because He is the one who knows the end from the beginning! More so He is the Beginning and the End, the Author and Finisher of all about goodness and grace!

## It Makes the Difference

It is not enough for you to see the invisible things because they do not have the power to sustain you during tough and rough moments on this road to your future. In addition to seeing the invisible, you have got to see the invisible One in whom all things hold together. He is the hope of the future when circumstantial evidences will be contradictory to the invisible things you saw. When you are able to see the invisible One in His faithfulness, grace, and power, an unwavering resolve will be born in you to hold on to truth by the power of faith.

About Moses, it is written that, *"By faith he left Egypt, not fearing the king's anger; he persevered because he saw him who is invisible."* (Hebrew 11:27) Seeing the invisible One produced faith in Moses, causing him to leave Egypt and persevere through the ordeal he went through for forty years in the wilderness.

Seeing the invisible One gives you a glimpse of His might and greatness, bringing a revelation of Himself as the One who works impossibilities. What you see in the invisible can motivate or paralyze you, depending on its magnitude. For it seems the things God has ordained us to accomplish are way beyond what we can do with our own strength, hence the need for a revelation of what He can do through us. Whatever God does is an extension of Himself. Seeing Him gives you an idea of what he wants to accomplish through you. God only reveals Himself to us in the capacity of what He has designed for us. No human being has ever or will ever have a complete view of the great Jehovah, Three in One, who spans eternity.

**He made it easier for us**

The Bible says Christ Jesus *"is the image of the invisible God…"* (Colossians 1:15), and, *"The Son is the radiance of God's glory and the exact representation of his being, sustaining all things by his powerful word."* (Hebrew 1:3 a) In other words, if you can behold the Son then you can behold the Father. Now, the Son is *"The Word became flesh and made his dwelling among us."* (John 1:14a). The word is here to give you a glimpse of who the Father is and what He can do in you and through you. The Spirit of God will show you things about the Father from the Word that will lead you to accomplish your future.

The Bible you have on your shelf is meant to give you a revelation of the Father by the Holy Spirit. It will reveal to you the character, abilities, and attributes of the invisible One. The Word is the road map to the future God has planned for you. When you neglect living according to Bible standards, you are neglecting God's ordained future for you. God wants to reveal Himself to you as the God of the impossible, and He wants to do that by His Spirit through His Word. When you are able to see the Lord as the God of the impossible, then that is a crucial step towards securing your future in God and with God.

**David Understood It!**

One thing that gave David a secure future was the fact that he was able to see Jehovah. As a shepherd boy, he saw the Lord as His Shepherd and declared in the most popular psalm, Psalm 23:

> *"The Lord is my shepherd, I lack nothing. He makes me lie down in green pastures, he leads me beside quiet waters, he refreshes my soul. He guides me along the right paths for his name's sake. Even though I walk through the darkest valley, I will fear no evil, for you are with me; your rod and your staff, they comfort me. You prepare a table before me in the presence of my enemies. You anoint my head with oil; my cup overflows. Surely your goodness and love will follow me all the days of my life, and I will dwell in the house of the Lord forever."*

Because David saw the Lord as his Shepherd, though he was a shepherd boy in need of love and acceptance, he was bold

*Seeing the Invisible One*

enough to declare that he lacked nothing. He prophesied abundance for his future by declaring that the Lord makes him to lie down in green pastures. He declared and proclaimed leadership and direction over his life by the Almighty God. Because he saw the Lord, he saw himself being anointed to the point of overflowing. And of course he became anointed as the king and functioned in the office of a prophet too.

David saw the Lord's goodness and mercy, so he could declare that goodness and love will follow him all the days of his life. God revealed Himself to David as a Shepherd because He had ordained David to Shepherd His people Israel. So when David was going through his ordeal in the hands of Saul, he was confident that God was going to see him through because he had beheld both the invisible and the invisible One. When you see and make declarations, your words become empowered by vision. Words alone do not suffice but words backed by a vision of the invisible and the invisible One become like immovable pillars in making the future established and secure.

This is another confident declaration made by David concerning his future:

> *5 Lord, you alone are my portion and my cup; you make my lot secure. 6 The boundary lines have fallen for me in*

*pleasant places; surely I have a delightful inheritance. <sup>7</sup> I will praise the Lord, who counsels me; even at night my heart instructs me. <sup>8</sup> I keep my eyes always on the Lord. With him at my right hand, I will not be shaken. 9 Therefore my heart is glad and my tongue rejoices; my body also will rest secure, <sup>10</sup> because you will not abandon me to the realm of the dead, nor will you let your faithful one see decay. <sup>11</sup> You make known to me the path of life; you will fill me with joy in your presence, with eternal pleasures at your right hand.*

(Psalm 16:5-11)

The only reason David could make such confident declaration is because his words were backed by his vision of the Lord. Verse 8 states, *"I keep my eyes always on the Lord. With him at my right hand, I will not be shaken."* David's eyes were fixed on the Lord, constantly, continually, expectantly, and habitually. He saw the Lord at his right hand. Oh, that your eyes may be opened to behold Him, that you may fix your gaze upon Him. Look at the details of the above declaration;

- You make my lot secure
- The boundary lines have fallen for me in pleasant places
- Surely I have a delightful inheritance
- With him at my right hand, I will not be shaken

*Seeing the Invisible One*

- My heart is glad and my tongue rejoices
- My body also will rest secure
- You make known to me the path of life
- You will fill me with joy in your presence

You see, David said his future was secure, he knew the path of life, had a delightful inheritance, a stable life, and a gleeful heart all because he had a vision of the Lord.

Let us pray:

> ***"Father, I thank you because you long to reveal Yourself to me, open my eyes Lord to behold You in Your power, might, and greatness. Lord, just as David saw You at his right hand, open the eyes of my heart to see You in Your Word, and know You for who You are so I may understand Your works and Your ways and therefore be able to step into the future with confidence and intrepidity, in Jesus' name, amen.***

# CHAPTER

# 3

## The Power of Your Vision

In the last chapter we said David's declarations were empowered by his vision of the invisible and the invisible One. Vision has the capacity to empower and invigorate a man or woman, boy or girl. Vision is power! Vision is strength! The man with a vision is one step closer to being unstoppable. Those who have succeeded to secure their future are those who have been able to see beyond the now into their tomorrow.

When the Lord wants to empower, He grants revelation. That is why the scriptures say, *"Where there is no vision, the people perish"* (Proverbs 29:18). Vision has the capacity to define boundaries and sustain a man in the face of adversity and uncertainty. Vision transforms the uncertain into certainty. It conceives the inconceivable, believes the impossible, and marches into the future with unfeigned boldness and resolve.

When you are in the midst of hopelessness, your vision will drive you out of the pit of disillusionment and despair unto the platform of hope and expectations. Vision converts cowards to courageous people, transforms weaklings to people of valor and might, and fills the fearful with intrepidity. Vision emboldens, enables, and enhances.

**God's way of empowering**

One of the ways God uses to transform and empower people is to give them a vision of the future He has in store for them. The problem is that many people are not attentive enough to decipher God's vision for them. This vision often comes in bits of coded mental imagery. It takes expectation to receive God's vision for your future. Expectations form the antenna that receives signals from God concerning what your future should be. When expectations are lacking, you become like a radio without any antenna. And though there may be an abundance of signals you will not be able to detect.

When the Lord wanted to show Abraham the vision he had for him in the future, he took him out of the tent and pointed to him the stars in the sky, and told him that was how his descendants were going to be. God likes to use imagery to speak to us and this is the way he showed Abraham his future. The Bible says, *"He took him outside and said, 'Look up at the sky and count the stars —if indeed you can count them.'"* Then he said to him, *"So shall your offspring be."* (Genesis 15:5) The Lord had told Abraham that Eliezer was not going to be his heir but Abraham did not get it until God took him out of the tent and showed him an image, that is, the stars. God explained to him that his descendants were going to be that numerous. It is then that Abraham *"believed the LORD, and he credited it to him as righteousness"* (Genesis 15:6) Vision converts skeptics to believers. It brings the unreachable within reach, and makes the unattainable attainable. It was the vision of the stars in the sky that produced faith in the heart of Abraham. God uses vision to generate faith in the heart of doubters and cast unbelief out of them.

When the Lord called young and fearful Jeremiah to the ministry, Jeremiah turned it down because he saw his own incapability as a young man. Nevertheless, the Lord decided to change his outlook by speaking to him through the power of vision. It is written:

> *"The word of the Lord came to me: "What do you see, Jeremiah?"*

> *"I see the branch of an almond tree," I replied.*
> *The Lord said to me, "You have seen correctly, for I am watching to see that my word is fulfilled."*
> *The word of the Lord came to me again: "What do you see?"*
> *"I see a pot that is boiling," I answered. "It is tilting toward us from the north."*
> *The Lord said to me, "From the north disaster will be poured out on all who live in the land. I am about to summon all the peoples of the northern kingdoms," declares the Lord."*
>
> (Jeremiah 1:11-15)

The Lord was giving Jeremiah a vision of the coming destruction so that through the power of vision he could be empowered to step into the future God had ordained for him before the foundations of the world. The Lord used vision to convince Jeremiah that He would sustain and protect him in spite of the opposition of Judah. The Lord was telling Jeremiah that if he could see rightly, then he would speak rightly and be empowered to do the impossible.

Joshua and the armies of Israel came face to face with the insurmountable wall of Jericho and wondered what would become of their onward march towards the Promised Land. To empower and encourage Joshua, the Lord gave him a vision of the commander of the LORD's army who then revealed to him the secret for conquest. Vision empowers you for victory and triumph.

Daniel, Ezekiel, Isaiah, and countless others were empowered by the vision God gave to them.

When Paul received a vision for Rome after the Lord appeared to him, nothing could stop hi from proclaiming the gospel in Rome. In spite of all the opposition, imprisonment, and intense persecution, the power of the vision sustained him and empowered him to overcome and triumph.

**A driving force**

The Bible says God has placed eternity in the hearts of men (Ecclesiastes 3:11). This is so that man will be motivated not by what is seen with the natural eyes but by what is seen with the eyes of the heart. Eternity consists of what is permanent or lasts forever. If you can lay your eyes on the unseen, then your motivation will come from a source that is permanent and reliable. And that is not farfetched. God has placed eternity within you, in your heart. If you can look inward, then you can see God's picture of your future, because He has placed it within you. When you become driven by eternity, by what the Father has placed within your heart, then will you be unstoppable.

## For the Joy set before Him

The writer of Hebrews, wrote, *"And let us run with endurance the race that is set before us, fixing our eyes on Jesus, the author and perfecter of our faith, who for the joy set before Him endured the cross, despising the shame, and has sat down at the right hand of the throne of God. For consider Him who has endured such hostility by sinners against Himself, so that you will not grow weary and lose heart."* (Hebrew 12:2-3)

His exhortation is for us to fix our eyes on Jesus, the invisible One. The vision we have of Jesus will act as a driving force for the pursuit of our future. You must learn to fix your gaze on the Lord. There lies one of the secrets to securing your future as we saw in the previous chapter.

Now the reason the Son of God endured the cross, and despised the shame of dying on that cruel tree is because of the vision He had. The Son's vision was a world reconciled to the Father's heart of undying love, a world free from bondage to sin, disease, addictions, and all forms of evil. He had a vision to see many sons and daughters being brought into the Father's family. He had a vision of His exaltation after the crucifixion and burial. His vision sustained Him through the cruelty of death on the cross. The vision was the *"joy set before him"*.

If you can have a vision of the joy the Father has set before you too, that will become a motivating factor to enduring all that is necessary to realize God's future for your life. You can secure your future by taking the first step towards that direction in tapping from the power of your vision.

Let us pray

> *Thank You, Lord, for the power of vision. Open my eyes oh Lord to behold the invisible. Give me a vision for my future. Help me tap from the power of vision so I can have a driving force for my life. Show me the joy set before me so that I may be empowered to endure anything absolutely necessary to realize the vision You give, in Jesus' name, amen.*

# CHAPTER

# 4

## Building Your Future – The Power of Prayer

One of the ways the Omniscient One has ordained for us to be able to secure our future in Him is by tapping from the preserving power of prayer. For many Christians, prayer is reactive rather than proactive. For you to effectively secure your future through the power of proactive prayer, you have to see the invisible future, behold the invisible One and allow yourself to be driven by the power of vision. The Lord lays the future in your heart so that you can pray it through to existence even though it will be made manifest in the physical at a later time.

Champions are people who are able to see from a distance, those who look ahead beyond the now. That which is not made secure through the power of prayer is susceptible to demonic interference and exchange. There are many people today who as a result of the neglect for proactive praying are living far from the future God ordained for them. What I mean is that, they never secured their future, and therefore the devil and his agents was able to exchange their destiny for something inferior to what God ordained for them. There are forces whose assignment is to divert destinies and destroy futures.

The writer of Ecclesiastes said, *"I have seen slaves riding on horses and princes walking like slaves on the land."* (10:7) The reason for this contradiction is satanic exchange of destinies. What is not secured in prayer becomes vulnerable to the wiles of the enemy. The princes assumed that because they were born princes, they were automatically going to ride on horseback, not knowing there were forces orchestrating changes before their future could come to them. Praying for your future is a way of travelling to the future and sealing it with God's power before any satanic interference.

The reason the Lord gives you a glimpse of your future by showing you the invisible, is so that you can secure it by the power of prayer. This is because, by the time your future is released from heaven by the Father to you, it has to go through the demon infested second heaven. There is high probability that forces that detect destinies will detect and divert the future that has not been secured through prayer. When you pray for things before they come to existence it empowers them to go through this satanic region undetected and unhindered. It becomes like a stealth vessel transporting vital supplies for an army in a war zone.

**Leave Nothing Unprayed for**

We said champions are people who see from a distance and are proactive rather than reactive. If you must live like the champion God created you to be, you must become proactive in praying for your future. First, if not already, you must pray for God to show you what He ordained for your future, that is, the destiny he planned for you. It is true that He may not show you everything at once but will show you enough to give you an idea of what it is supposed to be. Once you see it you can pray it with specificity. One of the secrets the Lord taught me earlier on in my Christian life is the need to pray for that which is yet to be.

What are the desires God has placed in your heart? What are the things you long to see happen? No matter how distant they may seem to be, you must understand that they are closer to destiny diverters in the spirit realm than they are to you. Things I prayed for several years ago are beginning to manifest in my life today. I travelled with God into my future and secured it with the power of prayer. I prayed for my academics, ministry, marriage life, financial life, professional life, and the different aspects of my future as I saw at the time. I spent time praying for the wife God had for me even before I was ready to get married. Because of this, even when I made very serious mistakes in the search for a wife, God worked it out for my good.

One of the prayers I made was to constantly grant the Lord permission to frustrate and destroy any pursuit of mine which was not in accordance with the future He had in store for me. Just one wrong move can distort the future. Nothing can divert your future like getting married to the wrong person or pursuing the wrong profession. One method of destiny diverters is to disorient you any way they can, and this often happens by setting you on course behind the wrong pursuits.

**How to pray**

First you must pray and thank the Lord constantly of the future he has ordained for you. Next ask Him to reveal it to you or at least give you a glimpse of what it is. He will do this by placing holy desires in you for some particular thing(s) or giving you mental pictures of your future.

Next you must pray and accept what you see, receiving it as a gift from God. Pray, protect it and hide it in the blood of the Lamb. Ask the Lord to block and frustrate every plan of the devil to divert or exchange or hinder your destiny. Now pray that every aspect of that future will come to existence at the appropriate time ordained by the Lord. Pray specifically for the things that need to come into place and into play for each aspect of your future to be realized. Do so as often as you can. In this way you will be securing the future with God through the irresistible power of prayer.

Let us pray

> *Father I thank You for the future you have for me. I thank You for making it possible for me to secure this future through the power of proactive prayer. Lord, as you show me aspects of my future, help me by the power of Your Spirit to secure the future through proactive praying. I refuse to be passive and let the future come to me without traveling to it through the Power of prayer, In Jesus' name, amen.*

# Chapter

# 5

## Building Your Future – The Power of Declarations

We have looked at the aspects of seeing the invisible, seeing the invisible One, the power of your vision, and building your future through the power of prayer. Now I will like us to look at building your future through the power of your declarations. I call this speaking to your future. Like I said before, many people let the future take them unawares without making any effort to influence it through God–ordained methods as we are outlining in this book. Your words have creative power, and there is no better way to use them as building blocks than speaking to your future – the purpose for which you were created. Just as your words can build the future God ordained for you, they can also tear down and destroy it. Your declarations or proclamations are never neutral, no matter how they may be.

**Watch Your Words**

One of the serious neglects of today's Christians is the responsibility of watching what they say about themselves or about their future. If you do not like the outcome then do not say it. The Lord God reprimanded Job by asking, *"Who is this that obscures my plans with words without knowledge?"* (Job 38:2) By your idle words you can hinder God's plan for your life. You can render murky the clear plans of God for your future by releasing words contrary to what He ordained for you. That is why you must be very careful about what you say about yourself and your future. It is the more reason you should long to have a glimpse of your future so that your declarations and proclamations are in line with the divine blueprint for you.

Job pleaded guilty to the Lord's charge saying, *"You asked, 'Who is this that obscures my plans without knowledge?' Surely I spoke of things I did not understand, things too wonderful for me to know."* (Job 42:3) If you don't understand it don't say it. If it is not in line with His word, don't say it. Nothing interferes with God's plans like speaking of things we do not understand. The secret to speaking right is to fill your heart with the word of God so that out of the abundance of the word in your heart, your mouth will speak. And when your mouth speaks the word of God, it is declaring what is in accordance with His plans for you.

**Declare the Future**

We said when declarations are made in accordance with what you have seen in the invisible and of the invisible One, they are empowered by your vision and can establish what is declared.

The Lord says, *"declare thou, that thou mayest be justified"* (Isaiah 43:26, KJV). Your declarations are able to justify the future God has in store for you against the accusations and intentions of the hosts of wickedness.

The Lord asks, *"Who then is like me? Let him proclaim it. Let him declare and lay out before me…"* (Isaiah 44:7) The Bible says we have been made in the image of God. More than that, it says *"…because as he is, so are we in this world."* (1John 4:17, KJV) So one of the rights we have because we are like Him is the right to declare things that are yet to come. Do you believe you are like Jesus in this world? Then begin to declare the things that He has ordained for you. You are risking your future when you fail to declare things in accordance with the divine plan for your life. Again the Lord says, *"Declare what is to be, present it..."* (Isaiah 45:21) Will you respond to that invitation? Will you begin to declare the things that are to be? Will you begin to present your case before the Judge of the universe? That is one of the ways to begin securing your future.

**In accordance with His plans**

The declarations you make must be in accordance with His plans for them to be effective. That is why you must see the invisible things and the invisible One for your declarations to be effectual. The Bible says, *"Who can speak and have it happen if the Lord has not decreed it?"* (Lamentations 3: 37) In order words you must declare what you have heard from His mouth or seen of Him. When you make declarations that do not originate from what He has planned for you, you interfere with His plans and obscure His counsel for your future. There is constructive power in making the right declarations and proclamations. And there is destructive power in the wrong proclamations.

Why must you make declarations only in accordance with His plans? Because in spite of all, what ultimately stands the test of time and adversity is what originates from the Lord himself! Throughout the scripture He has repeatedly stated that what He has planned will come to fulfillment. So to secure your future, you must declaratively build and establish it in accordance with His revealed will.

## God works in accordance with His plans

The psalmist said, *"Many, Lord my God, are the wonders you have done, the things you planned for us. None can compare with you; were I to speak and tell of your deeds, they would be too many to declare."* (Psalm 40:5) He saw the many wonders that God had worked in his life and praised the Lord for them. He said the wonders that God did in his life were too many for him to declare them. However, he acknowledge the fact that every one of the things God did for him and brought to pass in his life were all in accordance with His plan for him. The wonders God did were the things He planned for them. So one thing you must know and be sure of is that God will work wonders for you in accordance with His will for you as an individual, in conformity with His will for the universe at large.

Isaiah said, *"Lord, you are my God; I will exalt you and praise your name, for in perfect faithfulness you have done wonderful things, things planned long ago."* (Isaiah 25:1) God's faithfulness is in accordance with His plans. His wonders are in accordance with His plans. And these plans were established before the foundations of the world. Let your every declaration be in accordance with the divine plan for your life and you sure will see them established, and your future made secure.

## God is committed to His plans

For God's power to back your declarations about your future, they have to be in accordance with His plans. God is committed to see His plans established even as He ordained it. God is committed to His plans, and if the future you pursue is in line with His plans then He will be committed to building that future with you.

Isaiah said,

> *"The Lord Almighty has sworn, Surely, as I have planned, so it will be, and as I have purposed, so it will happen… $^{26}$ This is the plan determined for the whole world; his is the hand stretched out over all nations. $^{27}$ For the Lord Almighty has purposed, and who can thwart him? His hand is stretched out, and who can turn it back?*
>
> (Isaiah 14:24, 26-27)

If your future is according to the plan of God, things will happen according to how He has purposed them to be. So there is no need wasting your time, energy, and other useful resources to pray or make declarations which are not in accordance with His plans and purposes for you. God will stretch out His hands on your behalf to bring into existence His will for you.

Again the Lord says, *"From the east I summon a bird of prey; from a far-off land, a man to fulfill my purpose. What I have said, that I will bring about; what I have planned, that I will do."* (Isaiah 46:11) To fulfill your destiny, your declarations must be in accordance with the divine purpose. Your declarations must be in accordance with what God has said, that is, His spoken and written word. So, one of the ways to secure your future is to declare the written word of God over your life. It is my practice to declare what God has said in His word about me. As I make these declarations, I am bringing my future to align with what He has ordained, and therefore securing the future.

Let us pray

> *"Lord, thank you for giving me the ability to declare the future in accordance with your plans. Reveal to me your plans so I can use the power of declarations to secure the future. Fill me Lord, with faith and boldness to use the creative ability*

*of my words to establish and secure the future, in Jesus' name, amen."*

# Chapter

# 6

## Building Your Future - Declaring God's Word

One of the ways to be certain in securing your future is to declare the word of God over specific things that pertain to it. For example, I have used Psalm 23 to make declarations about my future. I have used it as follows:

Because the Lord is my Shepherd:

- I shall not want financially – all my financial needs shall be supplied
- I shall not want socially – I shall attain the social status ordained for me

- I shall not want academically – I shall rise to the academic level established for my future
- I shall not want spiritually – I shall live a healthy and devoted spiritual life
- I shall not want materially – all my material needs shall be supplied
- I shall not want emotionally – all my emotional needs shall be met
- I shall lie down in green pastures – spiritual, financial, intellectual, material, social abundance
- I shall live a peaceful life
- I shall walk the path of righteousness all the days of my life, and never tread the path of wickedness
- I will be confident when I go through difficult times
- The Lord will prepare a table of honor and abundance before me in the presence of my enemies
- My head shall always be anointed with oil
- My cup will run over spiritually, financially, socially, materially, etc.
- Surely, goodness and love will follow me every single day of my life
- I shall never backslide but will dwell in the house of God forever

I have also used Psalm 128 to make declarations about my future as follows:

*Building Your Future - Declaring God's Word*

Because I fear the Lord and walk in His ways:

- I will eat the fruit of my labors: physically, spiritually, intellectually and otherwise
- Blessings and prosperity shall be mine
- My wife will be a fruitful vine within my house
- My children will be like olive shoots round my table
- The Lord will bless me from Zion and in Zion all the days of my life
- I will see the prosperity of my Jerusalem
- I will live to see my children's children

For several years, I proclaimed, and am still proclaiming in accordance with Isaiah 14:24-27, and Isaiah 46:11 that:

- God's plan for me concerning ministry and service will stand and be fulfilled
- God's plan for me concerning marriage will stand and be fulfilled
- God's plan for me concerning academics will stand
- God's plan for me professionally will stand and be fulfilled
- God's plan for me financially and materially will stand
- God's plan for me socially will stand and be fulfilled

There are other things concerning the vision God has for my live for which I have been thanking Him and making declarations.

And as time passes I see them fall into place. I have also used Proverbs 31 to make declaration with respect to my future wife. My friend you can secure your future by declaring the word of God over it. Travel to your future through the power of godly declarations and establish things with God before you meet it. Be proactive towards your future beloved. You can also use passages like Hebrews 13:20-21 to make declarations of thanksgiving concerning your future. I have used it as follows:

- Father, thank you because you will equip me spiritually with everything good for doing you will
- Father, thank you because you will equip me financially with everything good for doing your will
- Father, thank you because you will equip me materially with everything good for doing your will
- Father, thank you because you will equip me intellectually with everything good for doing your will
- Father, thank you because you will equip me socially with everything good for doing your will
- Father, thank you because you will equip me with the gifts and talents for doing your will
- Father, thank you because you will equip me physically with everything good for doing your will

Now instead of making the declarations generally, you can include specific aspects of God's will for you in the declarations. The more specific you are, the greater the effect of your declarations, and the more established and secure the future becomes. That is why we started this book talking about seeing the invisible and the invisible One. He will reveal Himself to you in accordance with the future He ordained for you. So make it your goal to seek Him for specifics.

The above examples are only a few of declarations you can make about your future. Search the Word of God, and use Bible passages that have promises about your future and make declarations.

Let us pray

> *"Thank you, Lord, for giving me your word. Help me to make use of Your word in securing my future by using it to make declarations. Because You have said it in Your word, I know as I declare by faith each declaration will be established, in Jesus' name, amen."*

# CHAPTER 7

## Building Your Future – The Power of the Right Plans

We talked about the need to see the future, and the need to see the One who holds the future in His hands. We have also talked about the power of your vision, and the need to build your future through the power of prayer and the power of declarations. However, it doesn't matter how much you see, the extent of your vision, how much you pray and declare, if all these are not backed with the power of making the right plans, your future will be unsecured and will meet you unprepared. The right plans have the power to make you brave and ready to encounter your future.

## The Power of Planning

Everything being equal, you are only as secure as your ability to plan effectively. Many highflyers will tell you the secret to their success is the ability to plan. We have already emphasized the fact that all we do must be in accordance with His plans for us. No matter how glorious His plans for you are, if you fail to plan with Him, you risk forfeiting your future to the wind of carelessness. I like this particular verse of the bible that talks about the power of planning. Let me cite it from two different versions of the Bible:

> *"But the noble man devises noble plans; and by noble plans he stands." (NASB)*
> *"But the noble make noble plans, and by noble deeds they stand." (NIV)*

Plans are so important, when made in accordance with the will of the Father, they have the power to transform your vision into reality and translate what is in the invisible to the visible realm. No one ever truly succeeded without the power of proper planning.

## Our Supreme Example

Throughout the Book we read about the plans of the Omniscient One. I strongly believe part of His omniscience is His inherent ability to plan and follow His plans through. The bible says, *"But the plans of the Lord stand firm forever, the purposes of his heart through all generations."* (Psalm 33:11) If the omniscient, omnipotent, and omnipresent God who has the capacity to instantly create or speak things into existence makes plans, how much more of you and me?

God doesn't just make plans; He follows them through from generation to generation. In order word's He is committed to see every plan of His come to pass. So when you establish your plans with Him, and surrender your will to His, He will help you follow your plans through, since they are in accordance with what He ordained for you. We are exhorted to be imitators of God (Philippians 2:1). So because God is a planner, we ought to be planners with the only difference that we make our plans with Him, or in accordance with His revealed plans for our lives. Even then we submit the plans to His leadership and direction.

**The Power of plans**

We said before that our plans must agree with the plans of the Lord for our lives. It is impossible to secure the future by making plans that are contrary, or that deviate from the Lord's plans for you. The writer of proverbs says, *"Many are the plans in a person's heart, but it is the Lord's purpose that prevails."* (Proverbs 19:21) Hence no matter how many plans you make, or how well you make them, all your efforts will be futile unless they are in accordance with His plans and purposes. You do not want to waste time and other resources on things that will not become established, so plan with God, work with God, accomplish the plans with God. When you do that, you are upward bound for a secure future. Here are some benefits of planning:

- Success
  *"May he give you the desire of your heart and make all your plans succeed."* (Psalm 20:4)
  Until the desires of your heart have been translated into measurable plans, you cannot know lasting, thrilling, and true success. Job said, *"He thwarts the plans of the crafty, so that their hands achieve no success."* (5:12) In other words, success is achieved when plans are accomplished. When plans fail to be accomplished, hands achieve no success. And where there are no plans, there are no achievements and hence no success. So your plans will bring you success.
- Establishment
  *"Commit to the Lord whatever you do, and he will establish your plans"* (Proverbs 16:3)

> *"In their hearts humans plan their course, but the Lord establishes their steps."* (Proverbs 16:9)
>
> Your steps carry you forward into the future. As you make plans in your heart and write them down, as you step out to execute them, the Lord establishes your forward steps. But He has to see the plans in your heart. As you commit your plans to the Lord, he establishes them, thereby establishing your future. Your plans will bring you establishment.

- Profit

  > *"The plans of the diligent lead to profit as surely as haste leads to poverty."* (Proverbs 21:5)
  >
  > When you diligently make plans and execute them diligently, the bible says this will lead to profit. Plans lead to investments; may be of time, money, energy, and other resources. And your investments will always yield returns.

So, tap from the power of planning. Make long term plans. From the long term plans make short term plans. And from the short term plans, you can make measurable goals that can be evaluated at regular intervals. All achievers are first of all good planners. If you learn to plan, you will learn to fly high.

Let us pray

> *"Thank You Lord because You are the perfect example of a planner. Thank You for planning everything before the foundations of the world. Father, I want to tap from the power of planning. Teach me oh Lord how to plan and follow my plans through. Help me establish both short and long term plans in accordance with Your will for my life. Yet, make me flexible to adopt the plans as I receive more light from You, in Jesus' name, amen."*

# CHAPTER 8

## Sow into Your Future

We have explained the need to see into the future and to see the One who holds the future. We have exhorted you to tap from the power of vision, so you can receive a driving force into the future. Next we talked of how you can get into the future with God through the power of prayer. We also saw how you can begin building the future by using the power of declarations in accordance with the plans of the Most High God. Next, we discussed how to use the word of God to shape your future by declaring it. Lastly we discussed the power of planning in securing and establishing the future.

In this chapter we are going to see how you can secure the future by sowing in it. We are going to look at different ways you can sow in your future so that at the right time you will reap the mature fruits. By decree and oath the Lord established what he termed seed time and harvest time. In other words the Lord has established that as long as you sow and respect the principles that govern sowing and reaping, you are bound to reap. He said, *"As long as the earth endures, seedtime and harvest, cold and heat, summer and winter, day and night will never cease."* (Genesis 8:22) So, one way to ensure a future harvest is to sow in the present. Now let's look at some ways by which you can sow into your future.

**The Power of Your Seed**

You can identify ministries and ministers doing the work of God and sow seeds in their lives for the benefit of your future or specific aspects of your life. I have done this several times, and can tell you it works. There are many books on seed sowing. So I will not attempt to elaborate on that here. But the simple truth is you can secure your future by sowing seeds for specific things you want to see established. The only thing is you should be sure that the ground you are sowing on is fertile ground.

## The Power of Investment

The simple laws of economics teach us that proper and good investments are likely to bring good return, everything being equal. While I am not an economist or a financial expert to teach you on how to invest your capital, there are many other ways through which you can invest capital in your future. Man has been given several investment opportunities by God to invest in and secure his future. Here are some ways you can invest in your future;

## Develop Your Talents

The Lord has invested a wealth of natural abilities in you which we call talents. One of the simple yet very effective ways to secure your future is for you to invest in developing your talents. One of the ways the Lord has thought me to make huge investments in my future is by developing and employing my talents and gifts; both natural and spiritual. I started writing songs and poems several years ago. I wrote poems for individuals, especially my friends, on their birthdays and for seasonal greetings. I wrote poems and presented them in church and blessed God's people. I wrote songs which are yet to be heard by any human being on planet earth. There are many poems in my repertoire still to be read by any other individual.

I wrote about nine books before I ever self-published the first one. By the time I was publishing the second book, I had written over thirteen books. I kept investing in my future by writing. I put in time, energy, and effort writing what I did not know when it was going to be published. Sometimes the little money I had was invested to paying for the work to be typed and preserved. Someday somehow, I know the songs and the books will hit the market and bless hundreds of thousands of people, transform lives, and set destinies on course. Do not look for immediate returns. The folly of the men and women of this generation is that they are looking for instant returns. No huge investments bring any instant returns.

When David was developing his talent of playing stringed instruments, he did not know that was going to be the gateway to fulfilling his destiny. But there came a time in the future when someone was needed to minister to the king of the land, and David's talents or natural gifts made a way for him. This happened because he had invested time and other resources to develop the talent.

**Invest in Books**

Another way for you to invest in the future is to purchase knowledge and wisdom by investing in books. Books will give you secrets of high achievers shared in the stories of their personal lives. One of the areas I have consistently invested my money in is in the purchase of books, both academic and other books. As a boy growing up, there was a six year period in my adolescence when I had to work to support myself in school. What my father was making at the time was not sufficient to meet all our school needs. I left school sometimes and went to do odd jobs. I worked during the holidays and made some money.

As a youth there are several ways I could have spent my money. But I chose to invest it in the future by investing in books, and in my education. There is no pleasure you cannot have when you properly make investments for your future. The big trouble with many people is that they are squandering the seeds God has given them to invest in and secure their future. Read biographies and discover secrets and principles of success. Read, read, and acquire knowledge and wisdom. I can't understand how some people read but all they read is dirty novels that only help excite emotions and passions that should rather be left dormant. Invest that time instead on reading books that will benefit you now and in the future. In this way, you will be investing in, and securing your future.

## Train Yourself

You should train yourself both formally and informally. If you can, do all to get formal education to the highest level possible. If you cannot, then give yourself informal education by getting under the tutorship of one who has experience in your desired field. If you do not have the money to pay for that, you can do odd jobs and invest the money you have in what you want to become. Whatever it takes, give yourself some training; it will yield dividends for your future. Do not spend your whole time entertaining yourself with poverty and failure while giving others the little money you have. Have you not watched others perform enough? Is it not time to stop spending all your time in front of the TV or on social networks and do something useful with your time?

## The Power of Generosity

Another way, not too obvious to many people, by which they can sow in their future is through acts of generosity. No matter the little you have, you can consistently be a blessing to others by investing in their lives through acts of generosity. The bible says, *"Cast thy bread upon the waters: for thou shalt find it after many days."* (Ecclesiastes 11.1) When you give to people, you are investing in your own future. No matter how long it takes, your reward will come one day. Also, the bible says he who gives to the poor lends to God, and He will pay him back. Will you not want to lend to God? In due time, He will pay you back with interest. Sow in your future by blessing the poor and needy.

I am absolutely sure some of the favors I receive today are due to my generosity of the past. I have bought text books for people in the past. I have invested in the education of others and today such acts of selfless generosity are yielding dividends and they will yield more dividends in the future.

**The Power of Sacrifice**

Another great and sure way to invest in your future is through the power of sacrifice. Sacrifice will speak for you when and where nothing else will. When you enter the realm of sacrifice, you are entering the realm of a secured future. We could use countless illustrations to drive home this point, but let's focus on Ruth 2:10-12 for now.

Ruth found favor before the harvesters and gleaners in Boaz's field, and ultimately before Boaz, and she asked a very interesting question. The Bible says, *"At this, she bowed down with her face to the ground. She asked him, "Why have I found such favor in your eyes that you notice me —a foreigner?"*

Boaz replied, *"I've been told all about what you have done for your mother-in-law since the death of your husband —how you left your father and mother and your homeland and came to live with a people you did not know before. May the Lord repay you for what you have done. May you be richly rewarded by the Lord, the God of Israel, under whose wings you have come to take refuge. "* (Ruth 2:10-12)

The lesson we can draw from the above encounter about the power of sacrifice to help secure the future is that, selfless sacrifice never escapes the eyes of the ever-watching, all-seeing God of the universes. Anything you do to make someone else's life better is recorded by God and programmed for reward. Ruth's decision to sacrifice her safety, comfort, and *"future"* for Naomi moved heaven to grant her favor in the eyes of men.

Sacrifice is a magnet that attracts divine favor. Ours is a God who repays and rewards. Every act of kindness to God's beloved human race, and to his family in particular is record in the accounts of heaven for repayment and reward in due time. Sacrifice is the romance language of divinity. It is a fragrance that attracts divine attention. There are moments in life when the only thing that can speak for you is sacrifice, not present but past sacrifices that you may even have forgotten. Ruth's sacrifice to her mother-in-law spoke for her and gave her fa-

*Sow into Your Future*

vor in the land of Bethlehem. There are realms where only the voice of sacrifice has access and audience. Great sacrifices provoke great divine responses. And great sacrifices open great doors. Sacrifices are like bridges, elevators, and vehicles that carry you from one side of life, one level in life, one stage in life, to another.

You can sacrifice you money, time, energy, food, or other resources for the needs of others. You can also sacrifice your sleep, comfort, and good looks to invest into a worthy cause. Whatever the form of sacrifice, you must learn to employ and engage it in securing your future.

Let us pray

> ***"Thank You, Father for the power of sacrifice and its effect in securing the future. Lord I see the need for selfless sacrifice for the benefit of others. Help me Lord to make maximum use of the power of sacrifice to secure and establish the future, in Jesus, Name, amen."***

# Chapter

# 9

## Call Forth the Future

After building the future in the invisible realm by getting into it through prayer, declarations, and sacrifice, the next step is to call it forth to the realm of time. Calling forth the future requires faith, trust, and perseverance on your part. The greater your faith, the greater its effect in bringing the invisible future to the realm of visible time. Some people move to the level of calling forth the future before seeing, building, and establishing it in the invisible realm.

You cannot effectively call forth what you are a total stranger to, that is, what you have not seen, built, and planned for. Doing this will be like someone having a baby she is not ready to cater for! Adequate planning makes you ready to call forth your future after seeing and building. And remember that you see your future with the eyes of your heart, get into it by the power of prayer, build it through the power of declaration, planning, and sacrifice. Once all this is done, you are now ready to begin calling forth the future until it becomes reality.

**Activating Your Future**

I used the word activate because a man can only activate something that already exists and is ready for use. All what we have seen in the previous chapters was meant to bring your future to existence in the invisible realm. This very short chapter is meant to help translate the already existing, yet invisible future from the realm of eternity to the realm of time. Remember your future consists of the part of eternity close to being manifested in time, and the time that is yet to be. So how do you activate your future? The Bible says the God we serve calls into being things that do not exist. Let's look at Romans 4:17, from different versions:

> *"...even God, who gives life to the dead and calls into being that which does not exist." (NASB)*
> *"...even God, who quickeneth the dead, and calleth those things which be not as though they were." (KJV)*

## Call Forth the Future

> *"...in the sight of God in whom he believed, Who gives life to the dead and speaks of the nonexistent things that [He has foretold and promised] as if they [already] existed." (AMP)*
>
> *"...the God who gives life to the dead and calls into being things that were not." (NIV)*

God has placed in us His inherent capacity to call things into existence because He has called us and given us the ability to participate in the divine nature ( 2 Peter 1:3-4). The catch is that God sees before He calls them into being. He already pictures what has to be, how it has to be, and when it has to be. Then He begins calling them into existence by the word of His power. To activate your future, you've got to act as though you have already met it in the physical, and talk as though the future is right in front of you. Remember, God speaks of nonexistent things as if they already existed. This requires nothing short of or more than faith on your part, for *"Now faith is confidence in what we hope for and assurance about what we do not see."* (Hebrews 11:1) Your future is what you hope for; your future is what you do not yet see with the natural eyes. But you have to speak and act with confidence and assurance as though you were seeing it in plain sight. That is one way of activating your future.

A second way to activate your future is by the power of praying in tongues. Praying a lot in other tongues is not a ritual but a potent weapon to activate your future and carve out the way for your God ordained future to rush to you. Praying in tongues encodes your future and makes it possible for it to pass through the satanic territories of the second heavens and come to you unaltered. Praying in tongues empowers your future, and sets it on an unstoppable course to meet you in the realm of time. You can carve the path to your future by consistently, and extensively praying in tongues. When the power of unknown tongues is combined with the power of prayer, declaration, sacrifice, and planning, then your future becomes a no go zone for destiny destroyers. It becomes impossible for your destiny to be altered or exchanged for something else by evil forces. Your future needs activation energy and tongues will supply the energy needed to bring it alive.

Let us Pray

> *"Lord, thank you for granting me the privilege to be able to call into existence things that are not as though they were. Help me Lord, to speak and act as though the future you have for me is already here. Help me activate my future with the power of my words and the power of speaking consistently and extensively in other tongues, even as Your Spirit grants me utterance, in Jesus' Name, amen."*

# Chapter

# 10

## Celebrate Your Future

Another effective way to secure your future is by celebrating your future. Many people forfeit their God ordained future by failing to celebrate what God has planned for them. The question is how do you celebrate what does not yet exist in the physical, since we have been taught that celebration is for what you have accomplished? Well in a sense, since we are men and women of faith, and since you have seen the future, gotten into it, built and established it in the invisible realm, and are in the process of calling it into existence, or maybe you have already called into existence, then faith demands that you celebrate it. Celebrating the future is a way of saying *"here it is"*, or treasuring its arrival into the realm of physical time.

## How to Celebrate Your Future

### By prophetic thanksgiving, praise, and worship

One of the ways by which you can celebrate your future is by thanking the Lord for physical aspects of the future He has revealed to you. God is debtor to no one. As you consistently thank Him for what He has ordained for you, He will see to it that you enter into the fullness of everything you thank Him for, everything being equal. There is power in prophetic thanksgiving. Prophetic thanksgiving is thanking the Lord for His promises to you even before you enter into them. That is why you have to see the promises with the eyes of your heart.

You can thank Him for the ministry he has ordained for you in His body.

You can thank Him for the spouse and children or grandchildren He has for you.

You can thank Him for the spouse and in-laws He has for your children.

You can thank Him for your future vocation or profession.

You can thank Him for the businesses you are yet to establish.

You can thank Him for the doors that are yet to open for you.

You can thank Him for the partners He has in store for what he wants you to do.

You can thank Him for His provision of everything you need to translate into the physical realm what you have established with Him in the spirit realm.

Thank Him for everything possible and relevant for securing your future.

There is tremendous power in prophetic thanksgiving in securing and establishing the future you have created with God.

Another way to celebrate your future is to offer praise to the Lord for what is still to be made manifest. Praise Him for the manifestation of His power and greatness in bringing to pass what you and Him have established in the realm of the spirit through the process we have described so far. Jehoshaphat used the weapon of prophetic praise to defeat the armies that rallied against Israel. In that way he secured the future of the nation the enemy sought to destroy.

David secured his future by celebrating it through the power of praise and worship. The psalms are full of praise and worship of the Lord because David understood the power of praise and worship to secure the future. May your days be full of thanksgiving, praise, and worship to the Lord for the glorious future He has established for you! Gratitude will extend your latitude and increase your altitude when you maintain the right attitude.

**Delight in Your Future**

When you fail to delight in your future the tendency is for you to despise it. And of course, you and I know that you cannot celebrate what you despise. However, when you delight in your future you will celebrate it. Esau failed to delight in his future and therefore despised it. He sold it for a single meal and compromised his destiny. You have to delight in what God has showed you about yourself. It may not be as glorious as you want, but you must understand that God has the best interest for you than you have for yourself.

When you delight in your future, you will guard against compromising it. You will invest in it and nurture it to maturity. When you delight in your future, you value it above all else, especially above the gratifications of the present and the flesh. You evaluate the importance of things and activities by their impact on your future. You prioritize your life based on the future ordained for you by God. Celebrating the future will mean letting go of all that can hinder, delay, or divert it.

So now, you know how to celebrate your future, go tap from the power of celebration and bring your future to existence.

Let us pray

> *"Father, I thank you for the future you ordained for me. I confess that I will tap daily from the power of celebration through, thanksgiving, praise, and worship to secure my future. I will delight in what you have called me to be so that all else will be evaluated based on its impact on my future. I refuse to be carried away by the satisfaction of now at the price of my future. I refuse to be like Esau who compromised and sold his future. Help me Lord, to secure my future through the power of celebration, in Jesus' name, amen."*

# Chapter

# 11

## Surrender Your Future

From what we have said so far, it is as though everything about your future lies within, and depends entirely on you. However, there is an undisputable factor you must also take into consideration, and that is the sovereignty of God. In His infinite wisdom, God keeps working and co-ordinating everything in the universe to conform to His eternal purpose for mankind. It is for this reason that after you have seen, travelled into, planned, built, established, called forth, and celebrated, you must then surrender that future to the sovereignty of God. No matter how much you can see, it can only be as through a tinted glass. Paul said, *"For now we see through a glass, darkly; but then face to face: now I know in part; but then shall I know even as also I am known."*

(1 Corinthians 13: 12, KJV) So what you see is not the whole clear picture. Only God has seen the future as clearly as it is going to be. That is why you have to surrender it to the Lord. After doing all you are supposed to do in securing your future, you have to surrender the issue of time. Even as you planned it with Him, you have to execute it with Him, according to His time.

**Maintain the Desires**

Job in the midst of his trouble said *"My days have passed, my plans are shattered. Yet the desires of my heart turn night into day; in the face of the darkness light is near."* (Job 17:11-12)

There is the possibility of allowing the desires God has placed in your heart to wane and disappear into oblivion during difficult and trying moments. When the vision appears to delay, when plans appear shattered and crushed, many come to the point where they give up because they had not surrendered their future to the Lord.

Sometimes it seems the days have already passed and nothing you have seen, built in prayer and declarations, established and called forth, seems to happen. This is the time you should fan into flames the desires of your heart. Keep the desires alive. The desires of your heart will turn your night

*Surrender Your Future*

into the day of fulfillment of the vision. The desires will draw the light of day nearer in the face of the night of uncertainty.

David prayed, asking God to *"keep these desires and thoughts in the hearts of your people forever, and keep their hearts loyal to you."* (1 Chronicles 29:18) He was praying for the desire to do great things for God's house, the desire to see the temple built, and the kingdom established. You too can pray and ask the Lord to keep the desires in your heart until each comes to fruition. God wants to *"give you the desire of your heart and make all your plans succeed."* (Psalm 20:4) So you must keep the desires alive in the inmost part of your heart. Do not let them die. As long as the desires are alive, there is still hope that the plans for the future will succeed. When you delight in the Lord, and celebrate the future he has planned for you, and when you combine the celebration with desire, God will fulfill those desires. Never come to the point where you let go of your desires.

**Wait for the Lord**

Another aspect of surrendering the future is the capacity to wait for the vision to be accomplished. We said earlier that we must submit to the timing of the Lord, and wait for His plans to unfold. This is where the need for patience and perseverance comes in. When you fail to wait for the unfolding of His plans you risk ruining the future you invested so much in. Refuse to succumb to pressure from circumstances and hasten things according to your own timing.

Of the children of Israel, the psalmist said, *"Then they believed his promises and sang his praise. But they soon forgot what he had done and did not wait for his plan to unfold."* (Psalm 106:12-13) In other words they believed the vision God had for them, they even celebrated the future by singing songs of praise but soon forgot the good things the Lord had in store for them because of their inability to wait for the unfolding of His whole plan for their future.

Joseph saw his future many years in advance but he didn't know it was going to take him more than thirteen long years to meet it. He didn't know it had to take him down into the pit, down to Egypt, down to the dungeon before he would rise up to what the Lord had given him a glimpse of. So, be patient and wait, while holding steadfastly to the principles we have shared so far to secure your future.

David was crowned king several years before he became king. He had been given a picture of what the Lord had ordained for him. He had prayed, declared, and sacrificed to secure his future. Yet, it was several years before he could see it accomplished. However, fortunately he was ready for what he had been shown by the Lord. His future did not take him unawares. It only came later than he had expected, but the secret is he waited for it.

Both Joseph and David surrendered their futures to God, so surrender yours in order to learn to patiently wait, and certainly fulfill your future.

## Be Flexible

> *"Now listen, you who say, 'Today or tomorrow we will go to this or that city, spend a year there, carry on business and make money.' Why, you do not even know what will happen tomorrow. What is your life? You are a mist that appears for a little while and then vanishes. Instead, you ought to say, 'If it is the Lord's will, we will live and do this or that.'"*
>
> (James 4:13-17)

Even as you plan the future you must surrender it to the unfolding will of the Lord. Be flexible to adapt as things become clearer to you. Be ready to change plans as things unfold. Paul changed his plans at least once in the Bible. The Lord will test your obedience by altering what you thought you saw initially. You must be willing to submit all to Him. In that way you will secure your future. Be flexible enough to obey and follow His leading even when they seem contrary to what you thought you heard or saw. The God you are teaming with is a Master Planner, trust Him.

Let us pray

> *"Father, thank you because You are omniscient, and see the whole picture. Thank You because You coordinate everything in accordance with Your perfect timing and eternal plans for the universe. Lord, I surrender my future to Your hands and surrender every plan of mine to Your leadership and direction. Help me Lord to be flexible, yet maintain the desires You have placed in my heart even in the midst of uncertainties, in Jesus' name, amen."*

# Chapter

# 12

## Step into the Future

After all has been said and done, the best way you can secure your future is to step into it. Those who win don't only plan but step out courageously to accomplish their plans. The execution of plans is what I term stepping into your future. It will lead you to nowhere if you see, build, establish, call forth, and celebrate and you don't crown everything with practical steps to see your future fulfilled.

**Make Use of Your Opportunities**

Opportunities in life are like vehicles on divine assignment to motivate us to step into our future. Once we take the step, we can be sure that the omniscient, omnipotent, and omnipresent

One is there to lead and guide us unto fulfilling our future. Those who have accomplished their dreams are those who were willing to step into opportunities that were in the direction of their future. It's not every opportunity you should dive into. Some opportunities are just distractions from your desired future. That is why you should evaluate every opportunity whether it will lead you towards or away from your God-ordained future. However, because most opportunities give you only time for a split second-decision to get in or be left behind, you need to develop skills that will help you evaluate every opportunity with respect to its impact on your destiny.

Paul wrote, *"Be very careful, then, how you live — not as unwise but as wise, making the most of every opportunity, because the days are evil. Therefore do not be foolish, but understand what the Lord's will is."* (Ephesians 5:15-17)

Firstly, by this he was saying that in order for you to make maximum use of your opportunities, you must be careful the way you live. You cannot live carelessly and make use of godly opportunities. Secondly, he was saying you need to live daily in the wisdom the Lord has given you so as make use of your opportunities. Wisdom will help you make the necessary split second-decision required to maximize every opportunity. Thirdly, he was saying you need to have an understanding

*Step into the Future*

of the Lord's will so that you will make the most of your opportunities. When you maximize your opportunities you are stepping into your future.

**A Practical Example**

Take a look at Proverbs 31:10-31

There is so much practical counsel in the above passage on how to step into your future and make it secure. We will look at some.

**Look for something meaningful and profitable to work at:** Consider the example of the woman in the above passage:

- She selects wool and flax and works with eager hands V13 - **hard work**
- She considers a field and buys it; out of her earnings she plants a vineyard. V16 – **investment:** look for opportunities to make little investments
- In her hand she holds the distaff and grasps the spindle with her fingers. V19 – **handicraft:** use your talents and abilities to bring you income
- She makes coverings for her bed; she is clothed in fine linen and purple. V22 – **do not spend money on what you can do yourself**

- She makes linen garments and sells them, and supplies the merchants with sashes. V24 – **diversify your investments**
- She watches over the affairs of her household and does not eat the bread of idleness. V27 – **diligence:** do not waste your time doing nothing or doing things of no consequence

So my friend, step into your future by doing practical and profitable things that move you towards your destiny.

Let us pray

> *"Lord, thank You for making it possible to step into the future with you. Open my eyes Lord to behold every opportunity you bring my way to step into my future. Lord, help me to be careful, wise, and to understand Your will so that I will maximize my opportunities. Help me to make little investments that carry me towards my future, in Jesus' name, amen"*

# Chapter

# 13

## Avoid Dwelling in Kadesh

As you step into your future, there are places you must avoid dwelling in. On this road that leads to your future, some places you have to go through can stall or even destroy the future. One of such places is what the bible calls the desert of kadesh.

Usually, your present and your future are separated by the desert of kadesh. The distance, both in time and space, from where you are now and the future has a spot called kadesh, which you must not dwell in. Kadesh is meant to be one of those places you must go through to prove that you are worthy of the future God has shown you. It is the place where you make the choice between the present and the future, between pleasure and purpose, between investing and squandering, and between glorifying your creator and gratifying the flesh. At Kadesh you meet a crossroads of the highway of excellence and the dirty road of mediocrity, of the highway of holiness and the dirty road of compromise and indulgence.

The Psalmist said, *"The voice of the Lord shakes the desert; the Lord shakes the Desert of Kadesh."* (Psalm 29:8). This is because the Lord is not pleased when His people, on the way to their future come to dwell in Kadesh. He shakes the desert of kadesh to bring discomfort and discontent to all those who dwell in kadesh, so as to save their future from death and decay.

What then are the dangers of Kadesh?

### 1. The place of doubt and disbelief

The first time the children of Israel came to Kadesh (see Numbers 14:1-12), when the spies went into the Promised Land and surveyed it, they brought back reports that manifested doubt and disbelief of what God had promised them. Though two of them brought positive reports, the whole congregation took sides with the doubters. This is because at Kadesh people's hearts are inclined towards the negative than

*Avoid Dwelling in Kadesh*

the positive. So to make it to your future, you must avoid dwelling at Kadesh.

### 2. The place of delay

Another danger of Kadesh is that it is the place where everything that leads to the future is delayed. When you dwell in kadesh, everything about your future comes to a slowdown and eventual standstill. The Lord wants us to constantly progress towards the future He has ordained for us, but dwelling at Kadesh will bring us to a standstill. Moses told the young men who were now grown-ups, many years later that, *"And so you stayed in Kadesh many days—all the time you spent there."* (Deuteronomy 1:46) Kadesh can turn you into the direction of the past instead of the future (see Numbers 14:25)

### 3. The place of defeat

Another danger of kadesh is that it is the place of defeat. At Kadesh battles that were designed to be won are lost (Numbers 14:41-45). It is the place of defeat and therefore of resignation from the forward drive. Many people get stuck in a life of repeated defeat and failure for which no reasonable explanation can be given because they are dwelling at Kadesh. It is a place of defeat because it is a place of doubt and disbelief. On this road to your future, you need all the faith you can get. Anything or place that deprives you of faith sets you up for defeat. Moses told the children of those who had perished without realizing their future that when they came to Kadesh, *"The Amorites who lived in those hills came out against you; they chased you like a swarm of bees and beat you down from Seir all the way to Hormah."* (Deuteronomy 1:44) Kadesh is the place of defeat.

### 4. The place of death and decay

*"In the first month the whole Israelite community arrived the Desert of Zin, and they stayed at Kadesh. There Miriam died and was buried."*

(Numbers 20:1)

Another danger of staying in Kadesh is that it will lead to death and loss. When you dwell in kadesh your life will be filled with grief, loss and sorrow. In kadesh, dreams, potentials, visions, relationships and everything that is supposed to be alive for the future to come to you begins to die. In kadesh dreams are buried. It is also a place of decay because everything that dies has to be buried, and everything that is buried begins to experience decay. In the Christian life, everything has to be mobile in order to keep the life in it. Once anything with life in it comes to a prolonged standstill it begins to experience death and decay.

## 5. The place of despair

> *"They quarreled with Moses and said, 'If only we had died when our brothers fell dead before the Lord! ⁴ Why did you bring the Lord's community into this wilderness, that we and our livestock should die here?'"*
>
> (Numbers 20:3-4)

When you dwell in Kadesh, your hopes wither and the future becomes bleak and uncertain. Kadesh is a place that drains out any motivation for the future, and therefore despair creeps in. People who are in despair see only death around them. They feel like not moving on in life. It is the place of hopelessness and disillusionment. My friend, refuse to dwell in kadesh, avoid it if you can.

## 6. The place of deprivation

> *"Why did you bring us up out of Egypt to this terrible place? It has no grain or figs, grapevines or pomegranates. And there is no water to drink!"*
>
> (Numbers 20:5)

When you dwell in Kadesh, it is very likely that you will be deprived of the very basic and vital supplies essential for your march towards your future. It is for this reason that you have to avoid Kadesh, so that you can be constantly supplied with all you need to arrive at the future God ordained for you. The Lord has promised to supply all your needs, therefore, anytime you find yourself lacking your basic supplies, there is a very high probability that you are dwelling in Kadesh, for Kadesh is the place of lack and want.

### 7. The place of disobedience

> *"Take the staff, and you and your brother Aaron gather the assembly together. Speak to that rock before their eyes and it will pour out its water. You will bring water out of the rock for the community so they and their livestock can drink."*

So Moses took the staff from the Lord's presence, just as he commanded him. He and Aaron gathered the assembly together in front of the rock and Moses said to them, *"Listen, you rebels, must we bring you water out of this rock?" Then Moses raised his arm and struck the rock twice with his staff. Water gushed out, and the community and their livestock drank."* (Numbers 20:8-11)

For the very first time, we see Moses failing to follow the instructions of the Lord. Even Moses was caught in the trap of disobedience that lies in Kadesh. Kadesh is indeed a dangerous place. When you find yourself compromising the word

*Avoid Dwelling in Kadesh* 85

of God, when you find yourself constantly trying to bring the word of God to the plain of human reason and experience, you may have been caught in the trap of disobedience in Kadesh. Kadesh is the place of presumption and mistakes. All these will deprive you of the future the Lord has in store for you. The Lord later reminded Moses of this act of disobedience when He told him, *"for when the community rebelled at the waters in the Desert of Zin, both of you disobeyed my command to honor me as holy before their eyes."* (These were the waters of Meribah Kadesh, in the Desert of Zin). (Numbers 27:14) Kadesh is the place of disobedience.

### 8. The place of disqualification

*"But the Lord said to Moses and Aaron, "Because you did not trust in me enough to honor me as holy in the sight of the Israelites, you will not bring this community into the land I give them."*

(Numbers 20:12)

Because Kadesh is the place of disobedience, it is also the place of disqualification. When you live in disobedience, you disqualify yourself from the future God ordained for you. It is in Kadesh that both Moses and Aaron where disqualified from the future of entering the Promised Land because of disobedience. It is also in Kadesh that the Israelites of age twenty and above were disqualified from entering the Promised Land because of doubt and disbelief. So kadesh is the place of disqualification. When you choose to dwell in Kadesh, by default you are choosing to forfeit the glorious divine future for your life, thereby disqualifying yourself.

### 9. The place of disfavor

When the Israelites came to the edge of Edom, in Kadesh, they sent a request to the rulers of Edom for the favor to pass through their land, but Edom refused them the favor (Numbers 20:14-21). Twice they made the same request and twice they met with refusal, hence Kadesh is a place of disfavor.

One of the blessings that should help you accomplish your God-ordained future is favor before God and men. But when you are in Kadesh you lose that favor. When you are in Kadesh, you meet with refusal and rejection because you are clothed in disfavor. It is written in the book of Judges: *"But when they came up out of Egypt, Israel went through the wilderness to the Red Sea and on to Kadesh. Then Israel sent messengers to the king of Edom, saying, 'Give us permission to go through your country,' but the king of Edom would not listen. They sent also to the king of Moab, and he refused. So Israel stayed at Kadesh."* (Judges 11:16-17). Kadesh is the place of disfavor, and therefore of refusal and rejection.

*Avoid Dwelling in Kadesh*

You can secure your onward march to the future by avoiding kadesh. In case you find yourself in Kadesh get up and get out before death and decay take over your destiny. May the Lord shake the desert of kadesh that lies on your path, and may you be shaken out of kadesh by the voice of the Lord God, in Jesus Name, amen.

Let us pray

> ***"Father, I choose to follow the path you have ordained for me. Help me avoid dwelling in Kadesh. At every crossroad, help me to choose the highway of excellence, holiness, integrity, and hard work, instead of the dirty road of mediocrity, compromise, and indulgence. Lord, if ever I get stuck in Kadesh, I ask that you shake the desert of Kadesh so I may be shaken out of every form of complacency, in Jesus' Name, amen."***

# Conclusion

The future God has ordained for you is unspeakably glorious and delightful. To realize it you have to walk with God, and model your life in accordance with His statutes and ordinances. In case you have not yet established a New Covenant relationship with the God who ordained, and who holds your future, I want to give you the opportunity to begin that love relationship with Jesus Christ. He is the guarantee of your God-ordained future. Just pray with me with sincerity of heart and soul, say

> *"Lord Jesus, I know You are the Son of God and You are God the Son, I acknowledge that You died on the cross to set me free from sin and hell, and*

> *all the works of the devil and the flesh. I repent of all my sins and ask You for forgiveness and cleansing. Make me Your child and be my Savior and Lord all the days of my life. Take charge of my present and lead me into my God–ordained future, in Jesus' name, amen."*

If you made that prayer and are serious about the transaction that just took place, look for a Bible believing church and have fellowship with God's people. This way you will begin securing the future God has for you. Feel free to write and share with me your experience and I will be willing to help you as you seek to grow in this new life and secure your future. My contacts are on the front page of the book.

www.ingramcontent.com/pod-product-compliance
Lightning Source LLC
Chambersburg PA
CBHW020659300426
44112CB00007B/447